EMMET'S GUIDE TO BEING AWESOME

Fun tips, awesome advice, hilarious jokes, and more!

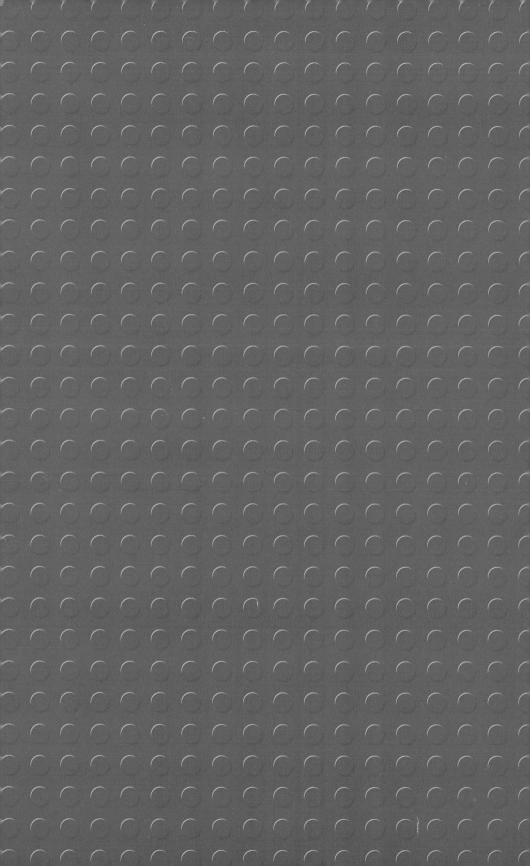

EMMET'S GUIDE TO BEING AWESOME

By Ace Landers

■SCHOLASTIC

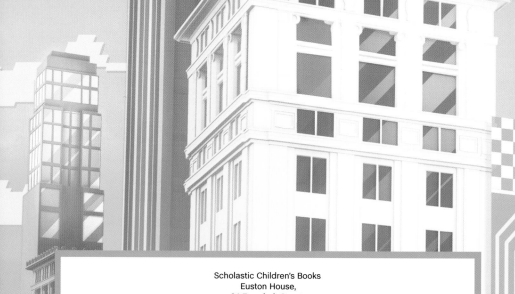

Scholastic Children's Books
Euston House,
24 Eversholt Street,
London NW1 1DB, UK

A division of Scholastic Ltd
London ~ New York ~ Toronto ~ Sydney ~ Auckland
Mexico City ~ New Delhi ~ Hong Kong

First published in the US in 2015 by Scholastic Inc.
Published in the UK by Scholastic Ltd, 2015

ISBN 978 1407 15645 3

Printed and bound by L.E.G.O., Italy.

2 4 6 8 10 9 7 5 3 1

Based on the Screenplay by PHIL LORD & CHRISTOPHER MILLER
Based on the Story by DAN HAGEMAN & KEVIN HAGEMAN and PHIL LORD AND
CHRISTOPHER MILLER.

Special thanks to Katrine Talks and Matthew Ashton.

CONTENTS

EVERYTHING
IS
AWESOME!

—EMMET

INTRODUCTION

Oh, hey! Emmet here. You know, that guy from
The LEGO® Movie. I'm glad you picked up this
book. We're going to have a totally amazing time!

That's because I'm here to show you how
to find your inner awesome. I know what you're
thinking: "He doesn't *look* awesome." And you
know what? You're right. I look totally normal.
And so do you (I'm guessing). But my friends,
the Master Builders, taught me that everyone
has the power within themselves to be special
and find their awesome side. And if I can do it,
so can you!

The People Who Taught Me About Finding Awesomeness

First, I should introduce you to my friends. Believe it or not, there was a time when I didn't feel very special. I didn't have a lot of experience leading or teaching or coming up with plans in general.

But then the Master Builders showed me how to believe in myself. They're the most creative people in the universe, and they can build anything out of anything!

Wyldstyle

Wyldstyle is super-smart and knows martial arts. She's pretty much the most awesome girl I've ever met.

Vitruvius

This blind wizard is the leader of the Master Builders. He taught me to trust my instincts. And to like cat posters.

Batman

Batman is a superhero. He's basically the definition of awesome. I think he actually *invented* awesome.

UniKitty

UniKitty is the happiest unicorn-cat thingy in the universe. She taught me that any idea is a good idea, except the not-happy ones.

MetalBeard

MetalBeard showed me that no matter how bad things get, there's always a way out. Like rebuilding your body out of pirate-ship parts.

Benny

And this spaceman is Benny. I'm not exactly sure what he taught me ... except that spaceships are cool. So I guess there's that.

Well, I think that's enough with the intros. Are you ready to discover what it means to be awesome? Me, too! Let's dive right in. We'll start at the beginning ...

EMMET'S GUIDE TO:

HAVING AN AWESOME MORNING

Rise and Shine!

Okay, sleepyhead, it's time to wake up. The sun is rising, the birds are chirping, and you never know what the day holds in store.

Here are some quick tricks to start your day off AWESOME!

Tip #1:

GREET THE DAY! I like to say good morning to everything around me, like my floor, my ceiling, my doorway, and most important, my hometown of Bricksburg!

Tip #2:

EXERCISE! Try sit-ups, push-ups, or parade marching. (Don't laugh! Those leg lifts really work your glutes.)

SIT-UPS

PUSH-UPS

PARADE MARCHING

EMMET SAYS:

My favourite exercise is jumping jacks. Hit 'em! One. Two! THREE! I AM SO PUMPED UP!

Getting Ready

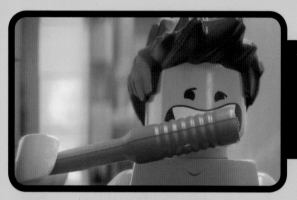

Tip #3:

BRUSH YOUR TEETH. It's hard to feel special when you have bad breath.

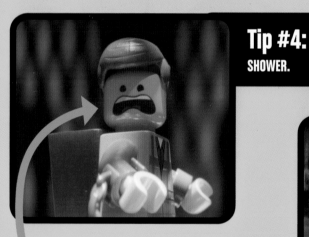

Tip #4:

SHOWER.

Aww!

A STINKY, SMELLY Emmet makes people feel like this.

A CLEAN AND FRESH-SMELLING Emmet makes people feel like this! See the difference?

Tip #5:

COMB YOUR HAIR. That way, you won't have to untangle a bird's nest hairdo every morning. You also won't have to worry about having a bird live in your hair.

Looking good!

Getting Ready

Tip #6:
DRESS FOR SUCCESS!

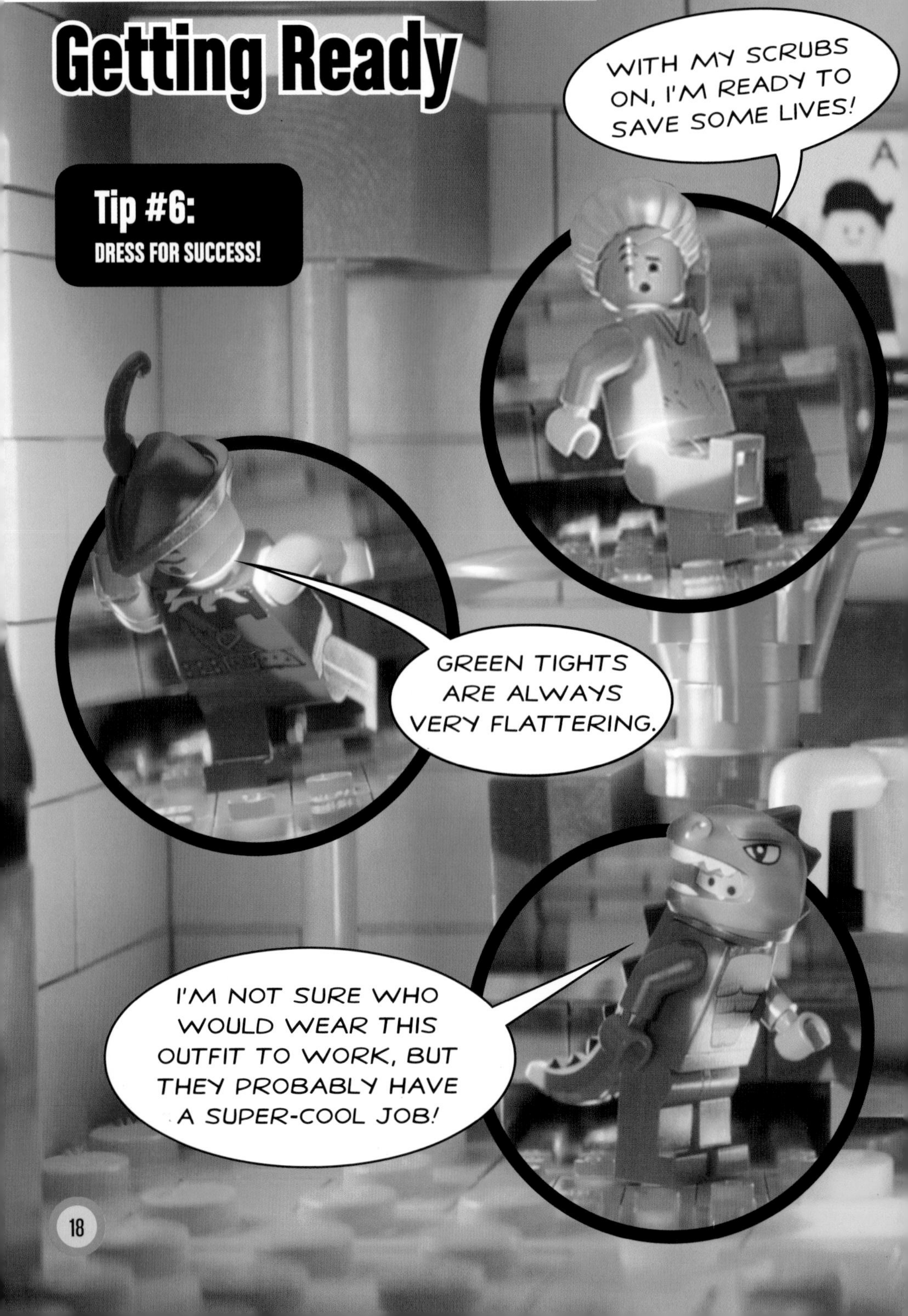

COME WITH ME IF YOU WANT TO *NOT* DIE.

–WYLDSTYLE

EMMET'S GUIDE TO:

MAKING FRIENDS

Just Say Hello

Making friends is easy-peasy! All you need to learn is one magic word: HELLO. You don't even have to be a wizard to use it!

Check out how these average Bricksburgians have mastered the art of "hello." They've even put their own personal spin on it.

SURFER DAVE

ALOHA, BRAH.

MRS. SCRATCHEN-POST

HI, FELLA.

MRS. SCRATCHEN-POST'S CATS

MEOW.

See? Don't you want to be friends with these guys already? Especially that cat. You can just tell he's cool.

Best Friends

But making best friends takes a little more time and effort. Sometimes when you meet a best friend, they might not like you. Wyldstyle didn't like me at first. Neither did Batman. Or a lot of the Master Builders, come to think of it.

But spending time together going on awesome adventures is totally how you make best friends! Take a look.

When Wyldstyle and I first met, I may have told her I was the most important person in the universe. She figured out pretty quickly I was fibbing and hit me with a cactus.

Friendship Fail!

But after escaping from Bad Cop in the Old West ... and Bad Cop again in Cloud Cuckoo Land ... and then saving the world from Lord Business ... well, it's hard not to be best friends after all that!

Batman thought my ideas were pretty pointless at first. But then my double-decker couch saved his life. Now we're totally BFFs.

EMMET SAYS:

Who are your best friends?
What kind of adventures do you go on?

Friendship Flowchart

Use this foolproof flowchart to practise making friends!
Choose yes or no to each question.

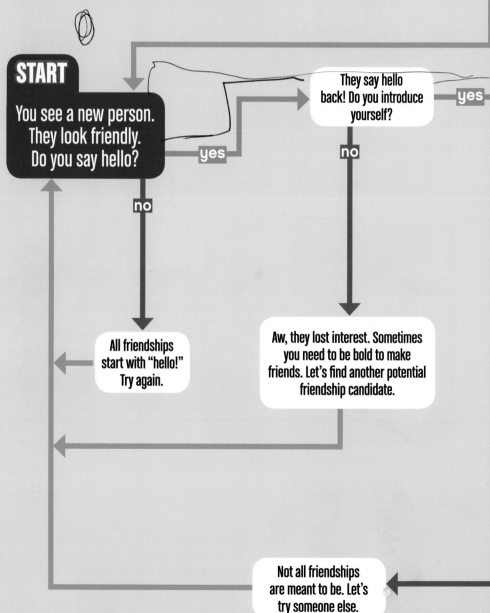

START

You see a new person.
They look friendly.
Do you say hello?

yes

no

They say hello
back! Do you introduce
yourself?

yes

no

All friendships
start with "hello!"
Try again.

Aw, they lost interest. Sometimes
you need to be bold to make
friends. Let's find another potential
friendship candidate.

Not all friendships
are meant to be. Let's
try someone else.

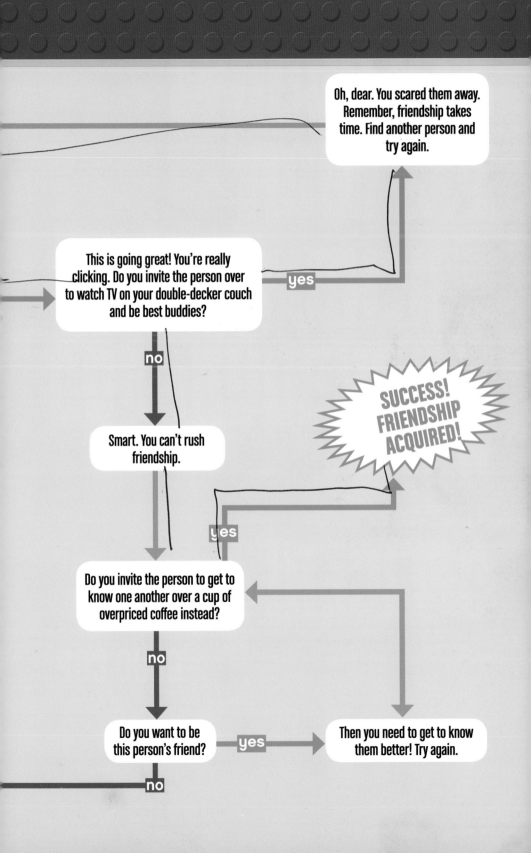

HEY BUDDY! I'M YOUR FRIENDLY NEIGHBOURHOOD POLICE OFFICER!
–GOOD COP

EMMET'S GUIDE TO:

DEALING WITH TRICKY SITUATIONS

AWKWARD MOMENTS

Let's just pretend this never happened . . .

SING
APARTME
FOR RE

From time to time we all find ourselves in awkward moments. Maybe you fall for Batman's girlfriend. Maybe everyone thinks you're the Chosen One. Maybe you suddenly realize you're not wearing any pants. (Okay, that one hasn't happened to me ... oh, wait, yes, it has.)

If this sounds oddly similar to your life, don't worry. Things are only awkward if you let them *be* awkward.

Am I being whooped by a bunch of evil robots ... or am *I* the one doing the whooping? Did that just blow your mind? Exactly.

How to Impress the Girl of Your Dreams

If you happen to fall for the most awesome girl in the world and you want to impress her, then you'd better be prepared to bring your A-game. Here are some heroic tactics that helped me:

Wow her with your **quick-thinking skills**, like using your head as a wheel axle. That'll get her head spinning for you!

Pick the perfect time to have a heart-to-heart with her. Like while dressed as a robot deep in the middle of an undercover siege.

Come up with cool ideas, like building a submarine to escape from Cloud Cuckoo Land. **DO NOT let Batman steal your cool ideas.**

Downplay the importance of dark and brooding songs. They're overrated.

DEALING WITH TRICKY SITUATIONS

Seriously, dark and brooding is entirely overrated! If you don't believe me, take a listen to Batman's latest song. Do you understand why this is art? I don't. But maybe it's just me.

"UNTITLED SELF-PORTRAIT"

A SONG WRITTEN AND PERFORMED BY BATMAN

DARKNESS

BLACK HOLE

MORE DARKNESS

THE OPPOSITE OF LIGHT!!!

CURTAINS DRAWN

IN THE BASEMENT

BLACK SUIT

BLACK COFFEE

[REFRAIN]

DARKNESS
NO PARENTS
SUPER-RICH
KINDA MAKES IT BETTER.!!!

WE'LL WING IT. THAT'S A BAT PUN.

—BATMAN

How to Handle a Super Villain

Life is filled with villains. They could be bullies or Brussels sprouts or that bird that chirps as soon as the sun rises until you wake up and can't go back to sleep.

NICE GUY.

LEAST NICEST GUY.

My villain was Lord Business. He seemed like a nice guy at first, but then we discovered that he was the least nicest guy ever. Stopping him was definitely one of the most awesome things I've ever done. Check out the tips on the next page for how I did it.

Tip #1:

Ask your friends for help. This is very important.

Tip #2:

Avoid fighting henchmen. Unless you're looking for trouble. If you *are* looking for trouble, then you should pick up Batman's guide to *Fighting Henchmen with Cool Gadgets.*

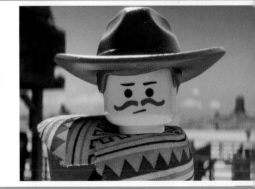

Tip #3:

Disguises! A painted-on moustache and an ill-fitting poncho can be the key to outsmarting a super villain.

Tip #4:

Always have a secret weapon. My secret weapon of choice is honesty. It's a bold move, but I've found it works. At least, 50 per cent of the time.

What to Do if You're the Chosen One

Sometimes in life, people will mistake you for someone else. As in, someone really, *really* important. Like the "Chosen One" or "The Special." That moment when you find out everyone thinks you're destined to save the world can be super-awkward. Here are some dos and don'ts I learned along the way.

THE CHOSEN ONE*

✗ DON'T: panic and/or freak out. You should at least try to act Chosen One-ish.

✔ DO: ask questions. As in, "Can you choose someone else?"

✔ DO: pay attention to the answers. You kind of need to know what the expectations are here.

✗ DON'T: fib about knowing you were the Chosen One all along. Even if the person you're trying to impress is really, really pretty. You'll just make them mad. And they'll hit you with a cactus.

✔ DO: be honest. It's okay to be nervous. Just don't screw up. As in ...

✗ DON'T: be brutally honest if you're giving a speech in front of lots of people. There's a delicate art to delivering the cold, hard truth with reassuring panache.

✔ DO: believe in yourself. After all, if you don't believe you have the power to be special, then how can anyone else?

✻ Label of "Chosen One" does not automatically guarantee super-abilities. Specialness must be found within and is subject to availability.

BELI

I KNOW IT
SOUNDS LIKE
A CAT POSTER,
BUT IT'S TRUE.

–VITRUVIUS

EMMET'S GUIDE TO:

TRAVELLING ABROAD

Greetings from Around the World

A big part of finding your inner specialness is travelling to new places. There's so much that the world can teach you. Let's visit a few of my favourite off-the-beaten-path locales and learn a thing or two about life on the road.

THE OLD WEST

Howdy!

MIDDLE ZEALAND

Fair tidings.

Cloud Cuckoo Land!

Wish you were here!

PRESIDENT
BUSINESS
OFFICE

Where your visit may run a little bit ... deadly.

The Old West

Well, howdy, partner. Welcome to the land of sand, where cactuses are spiky, moustaches are a must, and rowdy ruffians are always looking for a fight! Here are some helpful tips on how to blend in.

Bring your **ten-gallon hat**. Ball caps will automatically peg you as a tourist.

It's all about the **ponchos**, *mis amigos*. I look *mucho* snazzy, if I do say so myself.

Every cowboy worth his *yee-haw* has a **trusty steed** to ride into the sunset.

And if you're not into ponchos and moustaches, follow Wyldstyle's lead on being fashion-forward in the late-nineteenth century. Fans: the go-to accessory for keeping cool *and* battling robot sheriffs.

Rootin'-Tootin' Cowboy Lingo

If you're looking to really immerse yourself in the Old West culture, try out these handy-dandy phrases.

"Yee-haw!"
Translation: "Woo-hoo!" or "Excuse me, where is the closest outhouse?"

"Hands up!"
Translation: "Hands up!" If you hear this one, you should probably put your hands up ... or run. Or both.

"Howwwwdy! I'm a cowboy!"
Translation: "Good day to you, fine sir or lady."

[General pounding of fists in a saloon]
Translation: "That old-timey piano player is quite excellent."

And, fair warning, people here love to spit. A lot. Usually they spit into these things called spittoons. But all I'm saying is, if you're holding a glass in a saloon, keep a close eye on it.

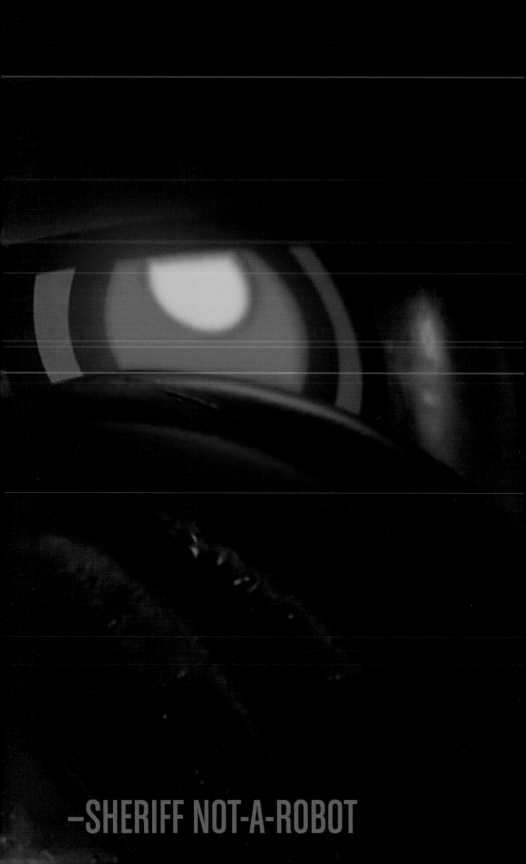

–SHERIFF NOT-A-ROBOT

Middle Zealand

The mystical land of Middle Zealand has everything: castles, knights, catapults, mutton, leeches, and DRAGONS! If you're planning a vacation here, don't forget your marshmallows. They're like catnip to dragons, or so I've heard.

Middle Zealand Dos and Don'ts:

DO: wear chain mail and a suit of armour.
It's heavy, but *so* sleek.

DON'T: swim in the castle moat.
It may look refreshing, but it's filled with all sorts of yucky stuff, like leeches.

DON'T: show off your fancy-pants reading skills. It will make the townsfolk jealous. And possibly get you sent to the stockade for practising sorcery.

DON'T: believe the brochures when they say castles are the best place to stay. Besides being drafty and dusty, the sleeping amenities take some getting used to.

Cloud Cuckoo Land

If the Dark Ages aren't your thing and there's a bit too much "old" in the "Old West", perhaps Cloud Cuckoo Land is the perfect getaway. Hidden high up in the clouds at the end of a rainbow, this is the happiest, most imaginative place in the universe. It's no wonder that the Master Builders love it here.

Cloud Cuckoo Land Rules:

Rule #1: There are no rules.

Rule #2: There is no government.

Rule #3: There is no bedtime.

Rule #4: There are no babysitters.

Rule #5: There are no frowny faces.

Rule #6: There are no bushy moustaches.
And above all ...

Rule # 7: There is no negativity
of any kind.

Rule # 8: There is also no consistency.

Rule #9: Any idea is a good idea
except the not-happy ones.

Rule #10: When in doubt,
refer to Rule #1.

Dos and Don'ts in Cloud Cuckoo Land

do Expect the unexpected. Dancing Dracula? A panda riding a snail? A mime painting a butterfly *on* a butterfly? That's just a Tuesday in Cloud Cuckoo Land!

do Prepare to be positive! I've always considered myself a happy-go-lucky guy, but I've got nothing on Princess UniKitty. She rules with an iron marshmallow.

do Marry a marshmallow if it asks you to. Just go with me on this one.

do Dress like a lizard or a clown when you attend a Cloud Cuckoo Land dance party. Don't forget your glow sticks.

don't Say the word *don't*. When in doubt, please refer back to Rule #1.

any idea is

except the
not-happy ones!

*unikitty

a good idea...

Octan Corporation's Super-Tower Headquarters

There are some places in life that you have to go, even if you don't want to. Lord Business's Octan Super-Tower Headquarters was like that for me. But if you ever find yourself stuck visiting a cold and ruthless villain's lair, here are some handy tips:

BRUSH UP ON YOUR ROBOT LINGO

"Business, business, business. Numbers."

Translation: "Concerning the sales forecast in the third quarter, let's synergize and square the circle so we can think outside of the box."

"Everything is awesome!"

Translation: This is the same in any language.

"Everything Is Awesome" is everybody's jam — even robots'.

"I'm here to see Your Tush."

Translation: There is a person, last name "Tush," first name, "Your," who is expecting a visitor.

BONUS TIP!
Robots are not programmed to understand silliness.

"Are you thinking what I'm thinking?"

Translation: "We should make photocopies of ourselves while no one is looking."

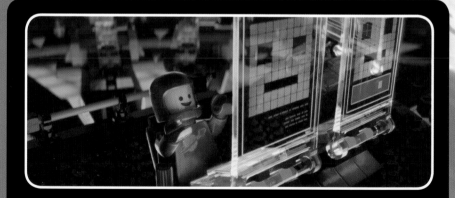

"Please disable the shield systems."

Translation: "Please initiate self-destruct sequence." Unfortunately, super-computers set up to protect Lord Business's headquarters can be tricky to operate.

NEVER PLACE YOUR REAR END ON A PIRATE'S FACE

"Take him to the Think Tank."
Translation: You should run. Now. Seriously, this is not a joke.
Hurry up, turn the page, and get out of here!

I JUST HAVE A JOB TO DO.

—BAD COP

DEEP
THOUGHTS

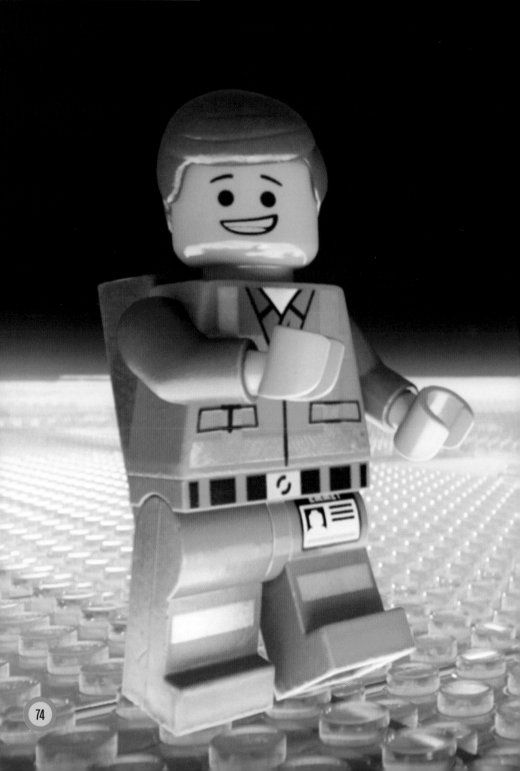

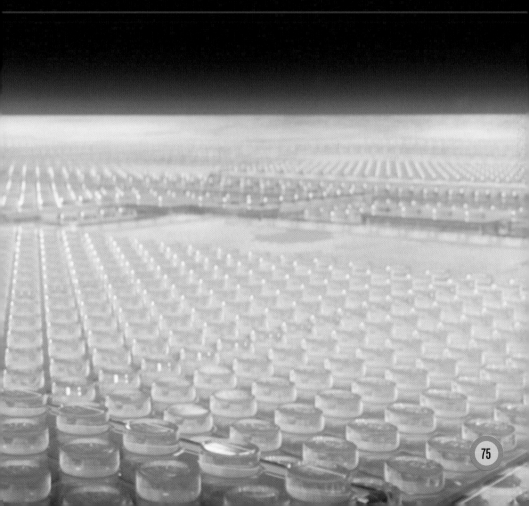

So far I've shown you some of my best everyday tips and tricks. But it's also awesome to spend quality time thinking about the mysteries of life. Like what's the real story with the man upstairs? Or how do the Master Builders know that all those parts to the vehicles they are building will fit together? Or *where are* the *Where Are My Pants?* guy's pants?! I've been told my brain has a lot of extra space, so jump on in and join me for some super-cool deep thinking.

WWWAMPGD?
(What Would *Where Are My Pants?* Guy Do?)

As I go through life's daily challenges, I often wonder, what would *Where Are My Pants?* guy do? I think it might go something like this:

- AT THE CLOTHING STORE: He'd buy pants, but then promptly lose them.

- AT A TOGA PARTY: He'd fit right in – no pants required! All right!

- AT AN IMPORTANT BUSINESS MEETING: He'd join via video conference. From the chest up.

- AT THE CLUB: He'd be a dancing machine. He's already danced his pants off! Get it?

- AT THE TRAVEL AGENCY: He'd book a trip to Scotland. Kilts are most definitely not pants.

Master Builder Advice

There are many lessons I've learned from my Master Builder buddies. Here are some of the deeper thoughts that they taught me on my adventure.

WYLDSTYLE (Lucy)

You don't need to have an awesome name to be an awesome person.

Good will always prevail, but you may have to get your face rubbed off by a bottle of nail polish remover first.

METALBEARD

Never scratch yer bum with a hand that's been replaced with a shark. This be very important.

BENNY

Do what you love and you'll never work a day in your life. Like building SPACESHIPS!

Unikitty

Always think positively!

ANGRY Kitty

PEOPLE NEED TO LEARN TO BE MORE FRIENDLY!

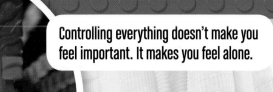

Controlling everything doesn't make you feel important. It makes you feel alone.

PRESIDENT BUSINESS

Anyone can be special if they just believe. Also, always protect your eyes.

VITRUVIUS

Anything is possible ... when you're Batman.

BATMAN

WITH PROPER TRAINING, YOU COULD BECOME A GREAT MASTER BUILDER

–VITRUVIUS

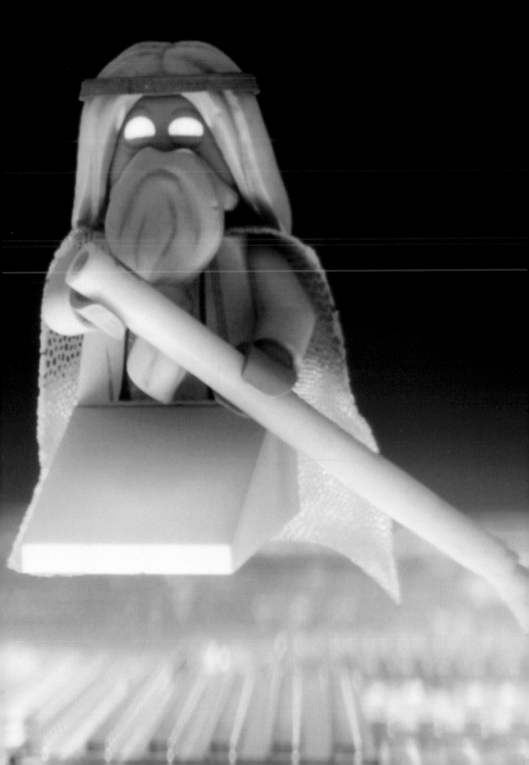

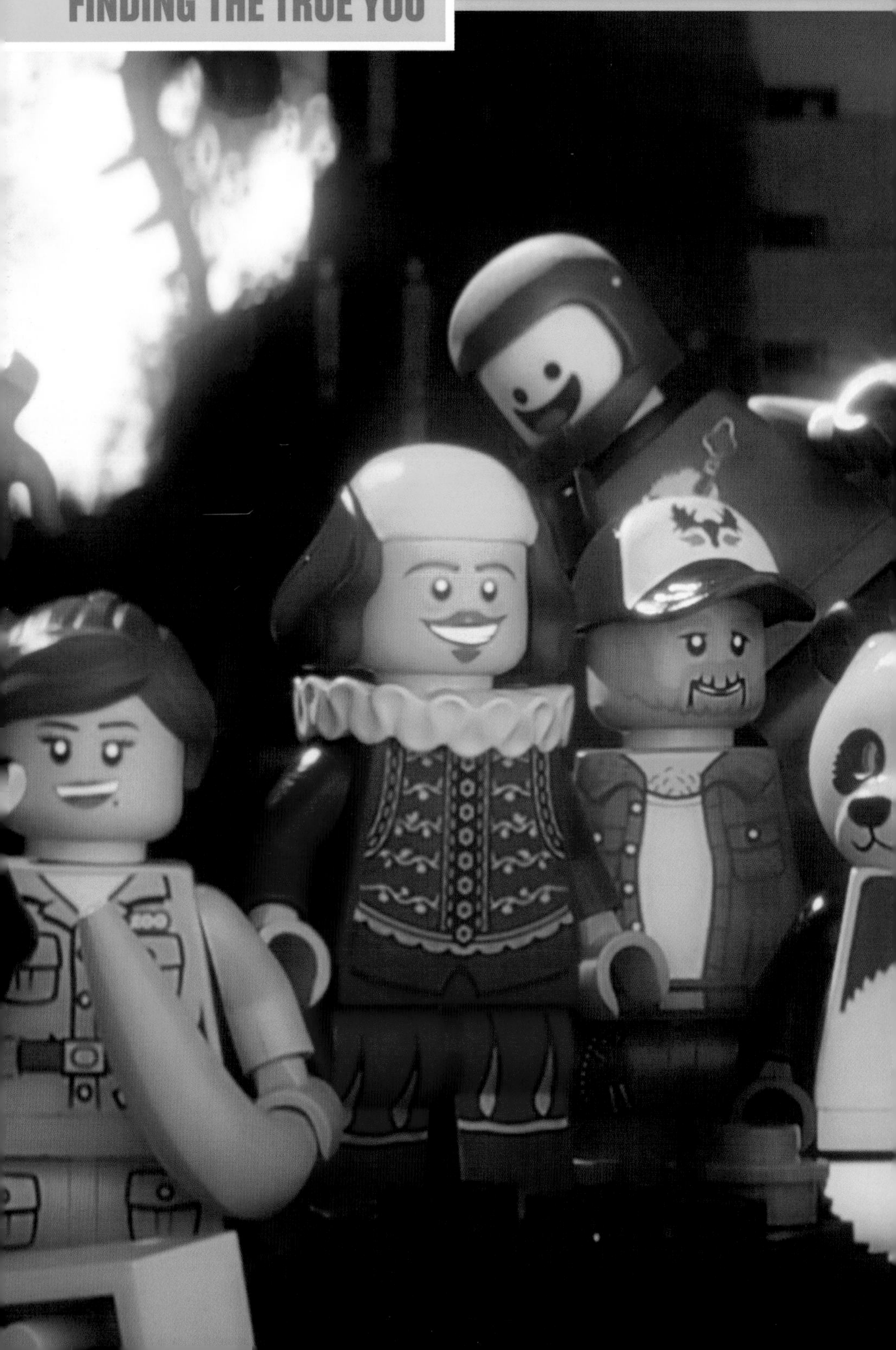

EMMET'S GUIDE TO:

FINDING
THE TRUE YOU

All right, enough about me. What about you? What kind of person do you want be? What kind of life do you want to lead? Read on to answer some questions that might help you better understand the true you.

Favourite Things

Now that you know a few of my favourite things, consider some of your favourite things.

Who are some of your favourite friends?
Surfer Dave? Mrs. Scratchen-Post?
Any of her cats, except Jeff; Ugh, that cat's got major cattitude.

What's your favourite song?
I mean, of course it's "Everything Is Awesome", right?

What's your favourite overpriced food?
Coffee? Chicken wings?
Sausages? Mutton?
Root-beer floats?

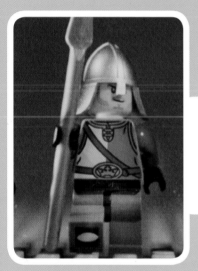

What's your favourite world?
Wait, do you even have
different worlds in your
world? Are you sure?

Who's your favourite superhero?
You've got a lot to choose
from. Batman, Superman,
Green Lantern, Green Ninja.
But if I could throw one more
name in the hat, it would be,
ahem, Abraham Lincoln.

LIFE QUIZ!

Which Master Builder do you relate to the most? Take this quiz to find out!

START HERE

Is there a side to you your friends know nothing about?

yes

no

Do you go by a secret name?

yes

Do you think caves are cool?

no

yes

yes

Are you just an average joe?

no

yes

Do you deserve to be the Special?

no

yes

Is what you do magic?

no

yes

Does Superman avoid you?

no

yes

yes

Are you sure?

no

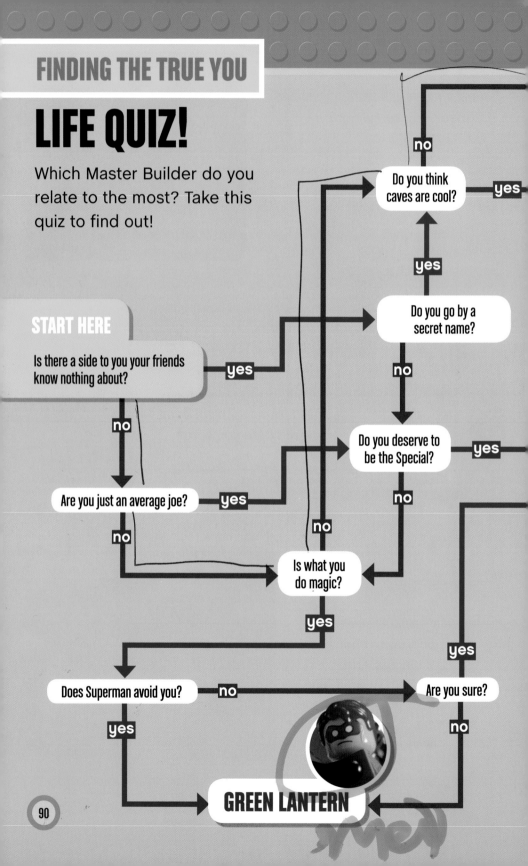

GREEN LANTERN

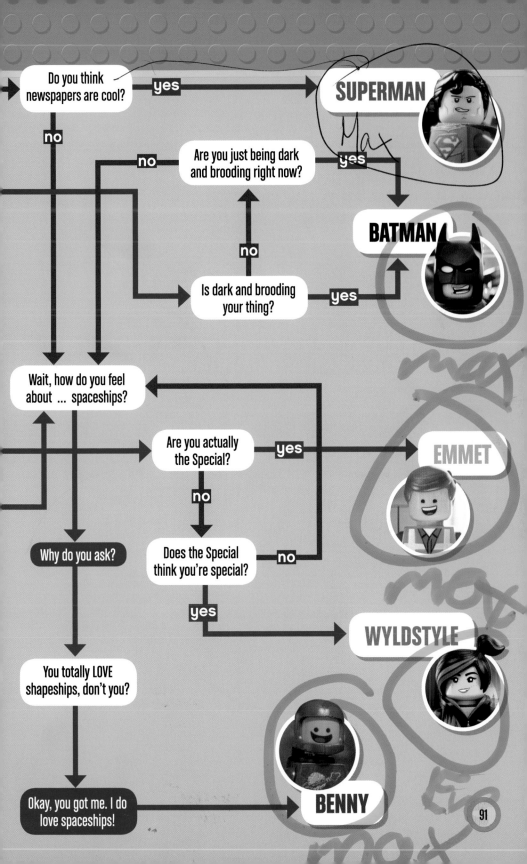

Do you think newspapers are cool?

yes → SUPERMAN

no

no → Are you just being dark and brooding right now? **yes** → BATMAN

no

Is dark and brooding your thing? **yes** → BATMAN

Wait, how do you feel about ... spaceships?

Are you actually the Special? **yes** → EMMET

no

Why do you ask?

Does the Special think you're special? **no** → EMMET

yes → WYLDSTYLE

You totally LOVE shapeships, don't you?

Okay, you got me. I do love spaceships! → BENNY

91

YOU ARE THE MOST TALENTED, MOST INTERESTING, AND MOST EXTRAORDINARY PERSON IN THE UNIVERSE.

10 Ways to Tell If You're

DO YOU:

1. Wear big-boy pants?

2. Tell people what to do?

3. Get super-frustrated when people mess up your stuff?

4. Use tacos as a means for mind control?

5. Surround yourself with robot minions?

6. Hatch evil schemes on a daily basis?

7. LOVE super-glue?

8. Control the entertainment industry and the government?

9. Like things to stay the same ... permanently?

10. Crave to destroy anything creative or different?

If you answered yes to more than half of the above, congratulations, you're an evil mastermind! If not, turn the page ...

FINDING THE TRUE YOU

Even if you're not an evil mastermind, I've found that the things we like say a lot about who we are. Select the relic from Lord Business's collection that speaks to you the most. What does it say about you?

KRAGLE

You are great in sticky situations and always hold it together. Most people see you as a fixer, but you can be stuck in your ways.

CLOAK OF BAN DA'ID

You are welcomed into new friendships at first, but it can be super-painful when it comes time to part.

SWORD OF EXACT ZERO

You are sharp and to the point - truly cutting edge.

PO-LISH REMOVER OF NA'IL

You exist to clean and your friends love you for it, but only in small doses. You also overpower the more creative people in your life with your no-nonsense attitude.

You are soft-spoken and gentle. People are always willing to lend you an ear.

FLEECE-CRESTED SCEPTER OF Q-TEEP

THE ORB OF TI-TELEEST

Hard-skinned, you can take a hit and keep on rolling. You belong to a lot of clubs, but ultimately you go where the wind blows.

IT'S NOT PERSONAL. IT'S JUST BUSINESS.

–LORD BUSINESS

What World Do You Really Belong In?

Take this quiz to discover your perfect realm! Choose one response to each question.

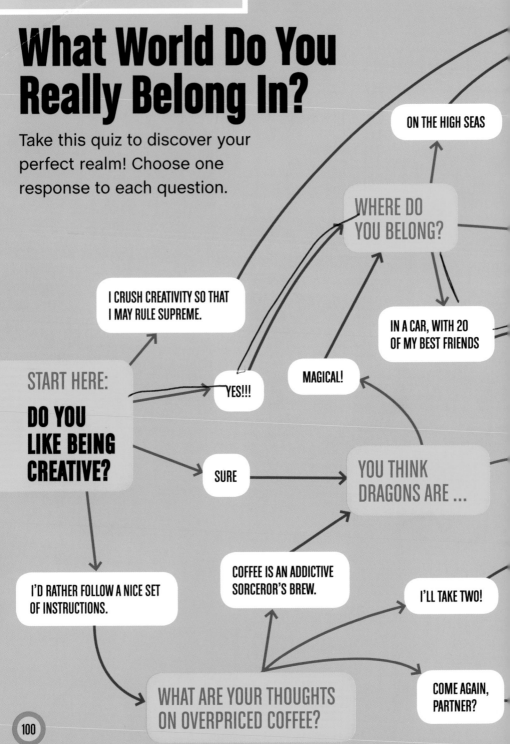

ON THE HIGH SEAS

WHERE DO YOU BELONG?

I CRUSH CREATIVITY SO THAT I MAY RULE SUPREME.

IN A CAR, WITH 20 OF MY BEST FRIENDS

START HERE:

DO YOU LIKE BEING CREATIVE?

YES!!!

MAGICAL!

SURE

YOU THINK DRAGONS ARE ...

COFFEE IS AN ADDICTIVE SORCEROR'S BREW.

I'LL TAKE TWO!

I'D RATHER FOLLOW A NICE SET OF INSTRUCTIONS.

COME AGAIN, PARTNER?

WHAT ARE YOUR THOUGHTS ON OVERPRICED COFFEE?

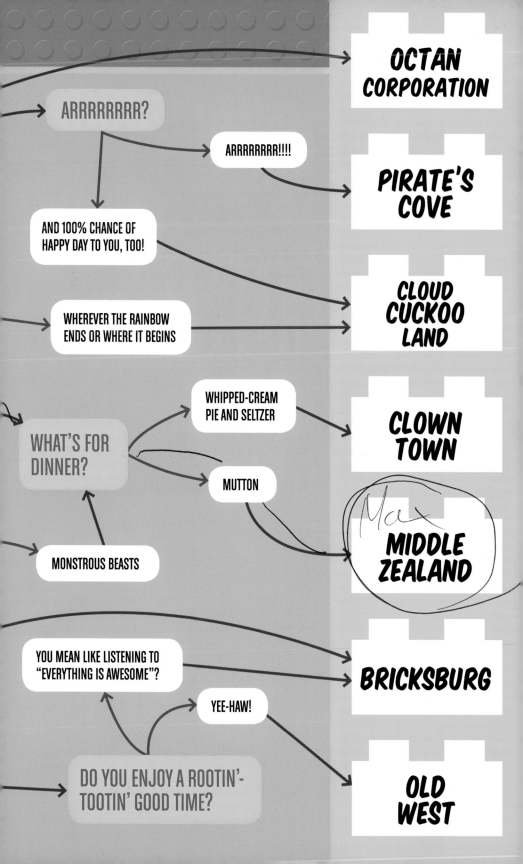

EMMET'S GUIDE TO:

FUN!

Totally Awesome Jokes!

If you want to be awesome, you should definitely know how to make people laugh. And there are only two things in my book that really make people laugh. Jokes and talking like a pirate.

Q: Why was Vitruvius afraid of boats?

A: They weren't "see" worthy.

Q: Why did Sheriff Not-a-Robot fall off his horse?

A: He lost his train of thought.

Knock, knock.
Who's there?
Interrupting pirate.
Interrupting pir—

AAARRRRRRRRRR!!!!

Q: What did Bad Cop say when he blasted apart Cloud Cuckoo Land?

A: Rest in pieces.

Q: What did Superman say when Lord Business captured him?

A: LEGO of me.

Q: How do you get a 1980-something astronaut to sleep?

A: Rocket.

Q: What do you get when UniKitty becomes angry?

A: Claw Enforcement

Q: What's Batman's favourite part of a joke?

A: The "punch" line.

Q: What kind of shoes does the Green Ninja wear?

A: Sneakers.

Q: What did one abominable snowman say to the other abominable snowman?

A: Are we there Yeti?

Q: What did the vampire say to the volcano?

A: I *lava* what you've done with the place.

Q: What do you call it when the Middle Zealand knights change places at the round table?

A: The knight shift!

Q: Why was Lord Business's robot assistant angry?

A: Because someone kept pushing her buttons.

Avast, Mateys! It's Pirate Time!

Talking like a pirate, while sometimes very important, can also be really silly. Here *arrrrr* some true piratisms to live by. Feel free to put several phrases together in one sentence to awesomize your pirateness!

"Ahoy!"
Translation: "Hello!"

"Avast"
Translation: "Stop"

"Aye"
Translation: "Yes"

"Booty"
Translation: "Loot"

"Come about"
Translation: "Turn the ship around"

"Davey Jones' Locker"
Translation: "The bottom of the sea"

"Fair winds to ye!"
Translation: "Goodbye, and good luck!"

"Fire in the hole!"
Translation: "Look out! Cannon fire!"

"Gangway!"
Translation: "Get out of the way!"

"Me hearties"
Translation: "My crew"

"Scupper that!"
Translation: "Throw that overboard!"

"Wiping yer bum with a hook for a hand be really hard."
Translation: "I'm not sure you've thought through this course of action."

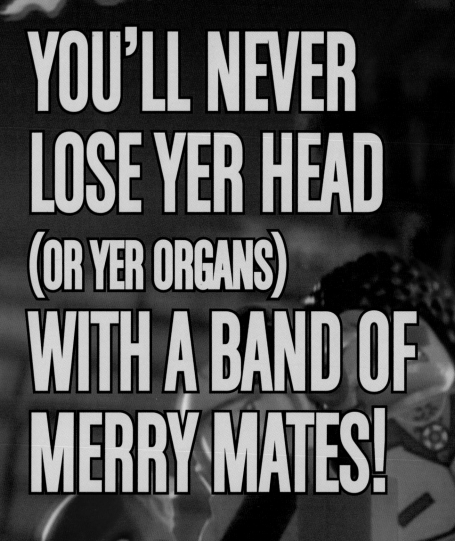

YOU'LL NEVER LOSE YER HEAD (OR YER ORGANS) WITH A BAND OF MERRY MATES!

–METALBEARD

EMMET'S GUIDE TO:

DOUBLE-DECKER-FYING
YOUR LIFE

Two Is Always Better Than One

By far, one of the most *awesome* ideas I had on my entire adventure was ... the double-decker couch! I mean, not only is it a really cool idea (who *wouldn't* want to all watch TV together and be buddies?) but it also wound up saving us from drowning. Who knew double-decker couches were buoyant?

That got me thinking – what else would be cool if it were double-decker-fied? The possibilities are endless!

Most Awesome

DOUBLE-DECKER CAR:
Double chance to call "Shotgun!"

DOUBLE-DECKER PIZZA:
Twice the cheesy goodness.

DOUBLE-DECKER BATMOBILE:
Oh my G.O.S.H.

DOUBLE-DECKER TELEVISION:
So you never have to choose between shows.

DOUBLE-DECKER VACATION:
That's a vacation on top of a vacation.

~~DOUBLE-DECKER HOMEWORK.~~
Wait ... never mind.

DOUBLE-DECKER PUPPIES:
Can you imagine the cuteness? And the mess.

DOUBLE-DECKER BALLOON:
If it accidentally floats away, at least it will have a buddy.

DOUBLE-DECKER PLANET:
Boom. Mind blown.

What else would you like to see double-decker-fied?
Try drawing a picture, or better yet, build it out of LEGO
bricks! That's what I did. And it was truly awesome!

HOW ABOUT ...
A DOUBLE-DECKER
SPACESHIP!

–BENNY

All Good Things Must Come to an End

And here we are, at the end of the book. Do you feel any more awesome yet?

Well, I do! We've travelled to different worlds, met all kinds of great friends, and learned all sorts of new ways to build totally awesome lives. But that doesn't mean the fun stops here. Each of us is special in our own way, and it's what you do with your talents that makes you truly awesome!

Check out the next pages for some great kick-starter ideas for more cool activities. And remember, they're all as awesome as you make them!

Emmet's Top-Ten Ways to Continue the Awesome!

1 Double-Decker-fy Something

Anything! Double-decker sandwich? Double-decker pillow fort? Double-decker LEGO building? Find something in your home to double-decker-fy and make it happen.

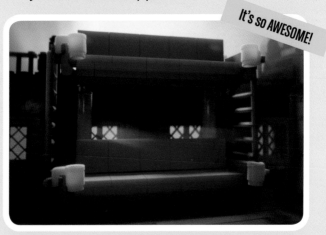

It's so AWESOME!

2 Song-Writing Challenge

Are you dark and brooding like Batman? Bubbly and creative like UniKitty? Write song lyrics that express the inner you, and crank up the subwoofers!

③ MetalBeard Body Switch

If you could replace any part of your body with something totally awesome, like a shark for an arm, what would it be? Make it out of paper, tape, and markers. Then wear it!

④ Power Suit

Lord Business thought he looked super-powerful in his red cape, evil-mastermind hat, and big-boy pants. If you had a super-suit, what would it look like? Draw it.

Big-boy pants.

⑤ Awesome Room Redesign

Vitruvius's apartment in the Old West was decorated very ... uniquely. Design something new to add to your room. Perhaps a funky LEGO mobile or a cat poster?

TURN THE PAGE TO CONTINUE CONTINUING THE AWESOMENESS!

6 Robot Dance Jam

Even Lord Business's robots couldn't help but boogie when they heard "Everything is Awesome" start to play. Make up your own robot dance and then jam to your favourite song.

THAT IS MY JAM!

7 Cloud Cuckoo Land Party

Host your own Cloud-Cuckoo-Land-themed party! This is pretty much an open ticket for anything goes. Want to dress like a dino? Go for it! Finger-paint with glow-in-the-dark neon paint? Do it!*

* Please do not finger-paint with glow-in-the-dark neon paint without a parent or adult's permission. If you are a parent or adult, please ask your child for permission to use his or her glow-in-the-dark neon finger paint.

8 Bat Gadgets (Patent Pending)

Batman has a cool gadget for every situation. Literally. Design your own awesome bat gadget. Remember to work in black and/or very, very dark gray.

9 Spaceship Build-Off

Benny loves space ... okay, you get the picture by now. Using LEGO bricks, challenge your friends to a spaceship build-off. First one to build the most awesome spaceship ever wins Benny's everlasting approval!

SPACESHIP!

SPACESHIP!

SPACESHIP!

SPACESHIP!

10 Write Your Own Awesome Adventure

Every adventure starts somewhere. Write yours! Where would you go? What would you do? Who would you meet and what evil masterminds would you battle? The only way to be the hero of your own story is to create it. Start now!

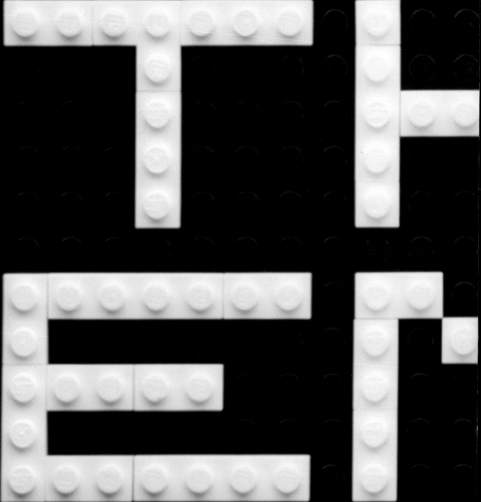

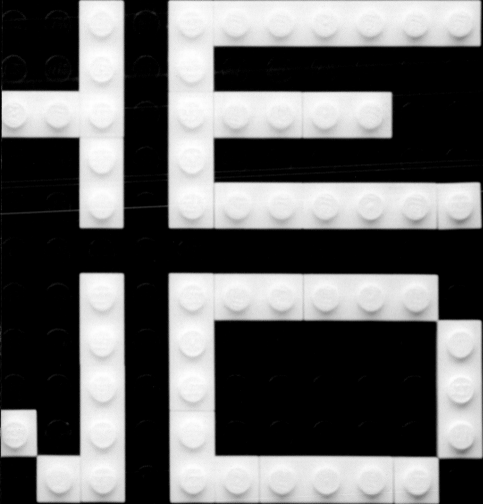